WHEN I OBSERVED HUMANS!

ITS ABOUT YOU...

YAKIN DIWAN

Copyright © Yakin Diwan
All Rights Reserved.

This book has been published with all efforts taken to make the material error-free after the consent of the author. However, the author and the publisher do not assume and hereby disclaim any liability to any party for any loss, damage, or disruption caused by errors or omissions, whether such errors or omissions result from negligence, accident, or any other cause.

While every effort has been made to avoid any mistake or omission, this publication is being sold on the condition and understanding that neither the author nor the publishers or printers would be liable in any manner to any person by reason of any mistake or omission in this publication or for any action taken or omitted to be taken or advice rendered or accepted on the basis of this work. For any defect in printing or binding the publishers will be liable only to replace the defective copy by another copy of this work then available.

I observed you and you inspired me to write...

I travel for the dedication...

Contents

Contents

Foreword

I maybe the one who wants to conclude something with a pen and a white sheet of paper "When I Observe Humans" and I think this gonna be something worth reading and even understanding it.

Apart from this, I won't take much time to in this but you must go onn and read it...

Preface

As I was a child I loved to travel and now as I am grown up a little I travel, travel doesn't mean the catchy places or any popular sites, travel for me just simply means going out of house, overcoming your boredom and observing the nature as well as humans.

Yeah till today I have travelled only two states in my life and I have plenty of things to tell you...

I even met different kind of people, their actions, their behaviour and was finding the truth about the humans.

Well I also have met someone special who inspired me more to write, its an intellectual property which won't be disclosed...

Apart from this and atlast I want to tell you to all my friends that its all about you, maybe your life, maybe your situations, just understant it in deep and try to go to the depth of the sea not on the surface...

I even write the poems in frustration or whenever I am upset, I just hold my pen tightly and we both just go onn....

I hope you all will like my poems..

Peace..

Takecare...

Go Ahead...

Acknowledgements

I just want to thank to all of you, you were all nice to me with no reasons, I hope I will be also supported with my poems too...

I want to thanks to **_Mewlana Jalaluddin Rumi_** for making me unnderstand to write and relate the nature....

And also a special thanks to you...

Prologue

Poems are the shortest stories with lots of explanations, I may not be the perfect writer but someone told me that if you are writing and delivering your emotions, no matter what its perfect for you and the person who reads it...

I hope you will all enjoy the poems....

Stay Blessed...

1. HOPE!

"*World admires you with a satire,*
People convince you with their proficience,
Nature proclaims you and you blame yourself,
You were born to provoke
But you are awaiting a stroke,
You have the scope,
And you are looking for a Hope...
- YAKIN DIWAN"

2. SUE!

"Those were the time back when I wanted to be with
everyone,
As the earth revolves time changes,
I'm right now in the darkness,
With myself and dealing with loneliness...
I hope the door opens up soon
And the brightness sues away the darkness...
- YAKIN DIWAN"

3. A Competition!

What happens when I see myself in mirror,
It seems that I have changed a lot,
The dedication which I had is lost,
The frustration I acquired has raised,
And a pale face had paved onn,
I was into the competition,
Competiting myself,
If I succeed, I failed,
If I failed, I succeed,
It was about "me" but do not try to relate it...

-YAKIN DIWAN

4. Scenario!

"We talk less or we shout aloud...
This happens when we are trapped in a cage,
To be patients of patience we show a rage,

A rage of courage or a rage of cowardness...
At the moment we are mentally ill,
And pretending to be righteous.

Living for assurance of life will deprive you from an
endurance,
And living to assure someone else's life will drive you
to precendance...
The act of selfishness will blow you up, And the act of
kindness will promote you towards yourself...
And I am waiting for a scenario to be chose...

-YAKIN DIWAN"

5. Heart!

"While holding a pen my heart went heavy,
Shivering and Shaking by the process,
Tightly knotted with notions going through my head,
And I started with the "heaviest part"...
Yeah! it went with lots of conspiracies and the
illusions,
Which leds to breakdowns and failures,
But it never betrayed and never failed to give voice
through stethoscope,
And still it beats with the same velocity...
Slowly it enlightened me and made me felt
lightheaded,
And a manifesto tries to convey that whoever you
are,
A heart will always be good with no reasons...

-YAKIN DIWAN"

6. What I can sense?

"*And you talk about what I can sense?*
I can smell fragrance of bad notions a miles away, I
can even see the changing face of "Moon" and even
the "Stars", And I can even observe those stones
which are now as soft as "Cotton",
I can even imagine that my first teachers would love
me eternally,
And to the conclusion with my senses, I can sense
everything but I don't want to ruin the journey...
- YAKIN DIWAN"

7. Which Road I took?

"*And the road I took now is under construction,*
Full of mist and frost, Non - Visibility opens up my
eyes,
And the droplets on the way energize me,
The cool breeze reminds me my good old days,
Alas!
I am not aware about the obstacles,
And whether I will be exempted from the road or
not...
I try to run away but it slackens me after I rest...
Atlast, I am not sure which road I took !!!
- YAKIN DIWAN"

8. Failure or Destruction?

“I ran away from my thoughts a decade ago,
An apocalypse was burning my soul and was in
search of an aid,
And overwhelming onto me and trying to play safe,
Wondering if it was a destruction or a failure!
I sighed
And a perception stucked me,
Failure can be cured,
And destruction can be stopped...
But which should I choose first...

That sphere was demolished.
Those gentles enjoyed their last day,
Those who were in love had lost themselves...
And those creatures had pale faces...
I observed and chose to stop destruction.

-YAKIN DIWAN”

9. Pretenders!

"I am in between the crowd,
Observing those who are feeling proud,
Its a only a day they will hold a shroud,
Again they will look for a scout,
And will couch infront of "Horde"...
- YAKIN DIWAN"

10. Reality is Fake!

"*We conquer demons, and we travel along with*
them,
We bribe them and we bet for the betterment,
We prohibit them from hurting, and we hurt them
for the instances,
We ask for the purity, and eventually we are dirty,
We are faked to be freed, and we are under realm,
We stay motivated and deep down we are dying,
We want our journey to be smooth,
And its just unreal...

-YAKIN DIWAN
"

11. I am on my way!

"I am on a way
In search of a reason,
To get over my passion,

I am on a way
With a prison,
To fix a treason,

I am on a way
To accomplish a mission,
With a sure vision.

Atlast!

I am on a way
Looking for negotiation
For a termination...

-YAKIN DIWAN"

12. Interrupt!

"PEOPLE WERE BUSY,
I WAS IN HURRY,

I RESPECTED AUTHORITY,
BUT SOMETHING ELSE WAS PRIORITY,

I SHOULD BE THERE WHERE I MUST BE,
THOUGH I WAITED UNTIL I CAUGHT RUST,

IT WAS TOUGH TO LEAVE,
AND THE REALITY WAS HARSH TO BELIEVE,

AT THE MOMENT,
WHEN I GOT A COMMENT,

THEY WERE ALL CORRUPT,
AND IT WAS BETTER TO INTERRUPT.

- YAKIN DIWAN"

13. Spirituality!

"In the world of Hate,
Am searching for Fate,

Trying to reach creatures,
And denying an instinct.

Realized about losing a treaty,

Fortunately,

Found a brook towards the faith...
And it incurred the spirituality from the soul.

-YAKIN DIWAN"

14. Soul!

"When I love someone,
I keep an eye on the essence of Harmony,
And I try to match the fragrance of the soul,
All that matters is a spiritual relations,
Afterall the only alive part of us is the soul...

-YAKIN DIWAN"

15. An Empty Brain!

"*Miles and miles away...*
In search of a "friend",
For wisdom and knowledge,
In a trauma to be lost...
Eventually,
Curiosity had stuck the soul,
Observations led to advice,
Necessities were expressed,
And the truth was delivered..
Still its an empty brain,
But to wonder ain't to be shock,
'Cos a learner is always incomplete...

-YAKIN DIWAN"

16. A Smile Holder!

"*Lots of happiness were burried,*
In exploring fantasies...

A smile holder was seen,
which was similar to an obvious Sunflower,
Energetic in day,
And calm at night...
Happiness was felt alive again,
And Found a way towards destiny,
For a testimony to treaty,
Lost in fragrance of smile holder...

Fictionally,

Was ashamed and perplexed,
Due to superiority,
Eyes were bowed without hesitation,
Thinking as its a demolition...

-YAKIN DIWAN"

17. The Demons!

"I KEPT MYSELF BEHIND A CURTAIN,

LISTENED TO THOSE SCHOLARS

WHISPERING,

IT WAS ABOUT A KNOWN,

I ACTED DUMB,

NEVERTHELESS!!!

I CAN'T RELY ON TALKS

AND PULLED OFF THE CONVERSATION,

THEY STARTED TO BELIEVE IN DEMONS...

AN IRONY, THEY WERE THE ONE...

-YAKIN DIWAN"

18. Me!

"I am self-owned,
Filled with the lights of all colour,
Filled with interests of all topics,
Filled with self humour, dignity and self respect...
I feel proud of me, until and unless I do something
wrong...
Though I am crazy, I am more mature...
Though I can show you my laugh when I am Sad...
I am motivated by self with a positive energy...

-YAKIN DIWAN"

19. Realization!

"IT WAS NOT A BIG DEAL TO IGNORE HER..
AND NOT EVEN TO TREAT HER LIKE NON,
YEAH, I COULD BE THE NONE,
BUT SHE IS ONLY ONE,
I WAS BUSY IN "ME",
STILL SHE REMAINED MINE,
SACRIFICED HER LIFE FOR ME,
EVEN WHEN I MISTREATED HER,
AND THE ONLY REALIZATION,
WHEN I SAW A DROP OF WATER AND IT WAS
HEAVY,
IT BROKE ME,
AND THREW ME IN MY BED...
THINKING ABOUT THE GOD'S PLAN,
WHICH FRUITFUL DEEDS GOT ME?
OR DO I NEED TO STRENGHTEN MY FAITH?
-YAKIN DIWAN"

20. SOMEHOW!

"When I ruin my own thoughts,
I blow myself and stuck
With a disease of overthinking,
When its time to be with everyone,
I start to isolate myself &
When I am unaware about me,
I start to talk and try to communicate
with my "Soul",
Though the soul isn't with me,
Though the soul stay away from me
but I just try to convince myself,
Somehow and Somewhere,
I get to stuck back with my own soul...
-YAKIN DIWAN
"

To Be Continued...

If you are till here that means you enjoyed reciting/ reading the poems by me...

I hope you have thought each and every lines in deep and didn't remained on the surface...

I hope that you will show some love towards my poems...

And I will also get a feedback regarding the poems on yakin.diwan1233@gmail.com

Thanks a lot!